Marcelo Henrique Santos

The use of games to attract audiences in the media

Marcelo Henrique Santos

The use of games to attract audiences in the media

In the book you will learn about the project that was developed for TV Galega (Santa Catarina)

ScienciaScripts

Imprint

Any brand names and product names mentioned in this book are subject to trademark, brand or patent protection and are trademarks or registered trademarks of their respective holders. The use of brand names, product names, common names, trade names, product descriptions etc. even without a particular marking in this work is in no way to be construed to mean that such names may be regarded as unrestricted in respect of trademark and brand protection legislation and could thus be used by anyone.

Cover image: www.ingimage.com

This book is a translation from the original published under ISBN 978-613-9-62089-0.

Publisher:
Sciencia Scripts
is a trademark of
Dodo Books Indian Ocean Ltd. and OmniScriptum S.R.L publishing group

120 High Road, East Finchley, London, N2 9ED, United Kingdom
Str. Armeneasca 28/1, office 1, Chisinau MD-2012, Republic of Moldova, Europe
Printed at: see last page
ISBN: 978-620-7-71248-9

SUMMARY

DEDICATORY

To God, to the patience of my fiancée and to my family for the opportunities and education I have received.

ACKNOWLEDGMENTS

To the companies TV Galega and Mauricio de Sousa Produçôes Ltda. who believed in the project and supported me in its development.

To Renata Abravanel, who believed in and invested in my potential.

To TVSBT Canal 4 de Sao Paulo S/A, Jose Carlos P. Almeida, Diego Felice, Keila Alves da Costa for encouraging me and allowing me to return to academic activities.

To my family members Carlos dos Santos, Neli dos Santos, Eunice Braz José Ribeiro, Reinaldo Francisco Ribeiro, Caio Cesar dos Santos, Berenice Braz José, Maiara dos Santos, who have always been by my side.

To my advisor, Prof. MSc. Murilo Garcia, for his dedication and direction in this research process and the elaboration of the project.

To Miriam Pereira de Andrade for her help and proofreading of the project.

To the teaching staff of this course for the lessons, debates and new points of view that have contributed greatly to my learning.

To my colleagues in the disciplines, for the conviviality and shared learning.

SUMMARY

Due to the huge market that digital games have been conquering, this work proposes the construction of some digital games with the common goal of serving as a vehicle for communicating companies' brands, strengthening their digital marketing strategies.

The aim of the games is to promote the company **TV GALEGA** (a television station from Santa Catarina).

To carry out the research, in addition to bibliographical material, material was collected from the respective companies.

Communication companies are looking for new media to stand out in the market and create differentiation strategies. Given this scenario, the companies interested in developing this work believe that their brands can reap long-term returns when they produce digital games to publicize the company and interact with the target audience.

Keywords: Television, TV Galega, broadcaster, games, digital games, digital marketing, online.

1. INTRODUCTION

This paper describes the process of developing four digital games integrated with the main social networks (Orkut, Twitter and Facebook) for the company **TV GALEGA**.

The company authorized the development of the apps (assigning the right to use images, logos, videos and audio) because it understood that *communicating* through digital games is a strategy to differentiate itself from the competition.

1.1 OBJECTIVE

The aim of this work is to present the stages in the development of digital games for companies in the communications sector, which can be used as a means of publicity to attract new customers and strengthen their brand on social networks.

1.2 METHODOLOGY

The development methodology for this work consists of the stages described below.

In stage 1, a bibliographical survey was carried out, using articles, books and publications, on the world of games, showing its structure, thus obtaining technical information and more in-depth concepts in the area of game development.

In stage 2, a series of conversations were held with professionals working in the field and/or studying it in order to create a project that could be used and launched later, resulting in a better understanding of game development in a practical way.

In stage 3, a study of the main social networks (Orkut, Twitter and Facebook) was carried out to enable the integration of games with these channels of dissemination and communication, resulting in a *case* that can be applied in future work.

In stage 4, the digital games were developed, resulting in a real example of the use of games to attract audiences in communication vehicles.

1.3 WORK STRUCTURE

The rest of this paper is structured as follows:

Capitulo 2: **DEFINITIONS ABOUT GAMES**, which presents the history and concepts about the world of games.

Capitulo 3: **GAME DEVELOPMENT**, where concepts about game development ideas, target audience definition, planning and game design are presented.

Capitulo 4: **TV GALEGA PROJECT**, which presents the company's profile, documentation and the study carried out to develop the game.

Capitulo 5: **CONCLUSION**, where the conclusions of the work and proposals for its continuation are presented.

Capitulo 6: **ANNEXES**, where copies of the contracts authorizing the use of images, logos, audio and photos of the media companies (TV Galega) and excerpts from the source codes are presented.

2. DEFINITIONS OF GAMES

According to Huizinga (1993, p.16), we can highlight some characteristics of the game that help in the attempt to formulate a concept. According to him, the game is a "free activity, consciously taken as 'non-serious' and external to normal life, but at the same time capable of absorbing the player in an intense and total way".

Play is a behavior identified in both animals and humans, "it is more than a physiological phenomenon or a psychological reflex. It goes beyond the limits of purely physical or biological activity. It is a signifier, that is, it contains a certain meaning". (HUIZINGA, 1993, p.4)

A game is a voluntary activity or occupation, carried out within certain limits of time and space, according to rules that are freely consented to but absolutely obligatory, with an end in itself, accompanied by a feeling of tension and joy and an awareness of being different from everyday life. (HUIZINGA, 1993, p.33)

According to Crawford (1982, p. 169), games can be divided into: board games, card games, athletic games, children's games and computer games. Crawford further defines games as :

A collection of parts that interact with each other, often in complex ways (CRAWFORD, 1982, p. 169).

2.1 GAMES MARKET

To give you an idea, the video game segment in the United States, the largest in the world, had a total turnover in 2005, including the sale of games and equipment, of 10.5 billion dollars, compared to 9 billion for the film industry. (MISTERAPE, 2006, p. 39)

According to the research, the history of the Brazilian games industry is older than you might think, as there has been an attempt to penetrate this market since the 1980s. The first companies appeared in 1992, but it was in 1997 that the market began to grow strongly and in 1999 Brazil had a record number of companies founded (21% of the total). At the time of the study, 55 active developers were registered (ABRAGAMES, 2005).

The games market in Brazil was segmented into niches. The majority of companies focused on the traditional entertainment market (72%), but there was a growing interest in *advergames* (games with an advertising slant) and the start of production of *business games* (business simulations aimed at learning) and *middleware* (a tool needed for the process of developing and maintaining games). According to Jairo Margatho, marketing manager at developer Délirus Entertainment, advertising agencies already recognize *advergames as* an interactive media that has a potential audience that spends at least four hours on the computer (ABRAGAMES, 2005).

In this context, most companies focused on the PC platform (63%) and secondly on cell phones (22%). According to Tarqüinio Teles, president and marketing director of developer Hoplon Infotainment, this is because programmers' knowledge, acquired at university, is still geared towards the PC. The growing investment in the production of mobile games is mainly due to the inhibition of piracy brought about by new technologies. As for the large console market, the difficulty in obtaining licenses for development kits is still great, which prevents Brazilian developers from penetrating this field. Without official distribution, there is also no support or incentive. One of the obstacles to this scenario changing is piracy in the country, which, according to a study by IDG Consulting in 2004, was around 94% and caused losses of around 210 million dollars (ABRAGAMES, 2005).

2.2 DIGITAL MARKETING

Digital marketing technology helps to understand who the *prospects* are and what they want. It provides the visibility needed for the company to be appreciated by customers and enables the business to improve its results and consequently generate more profit. (CUNHA, 2011, p. 54)

Digital Marketing Actions is a communication process that uses the resources of the digital medium (currently the most widely used is through the internet and will be presented throughout the work), which makes it possible to treat the customer with a unique and direct language.

2.3 WEB 2.0

In Web 1.0, the pages were static and did not allow the content to be modified. Based on HTML codes, this version referred to the relationship between man and machine in which interactivity and participation in the construction of information were limited. Web 2.0, on the other hand, brings a new generation of services and applications responsible for changes in user habits within the virtual space. This profile is based on collaborative content built and modified by the users themselves, as well as increasingly strong integration between sites and services (machine to machine). (TARCIA, 2007, p.19)

"The term Web 2.0 is used to describe the second generation of the World Wide Web, a trend that reinforces the concept of information exchange and collaboration between internet users and virtual sites and services. The idea is for the online environment to become more dynamic and for users to collaborate in organizing content." (Folha Online 2006)

For Pereira (2006), the new concept of the Web is not a revolution, it's just an evolution. This virtual reality is a marketing ploy by companies and professionals who want to sell new technologies. According to him, there is nothing extraordinary about these "new" programs and this term has arisen because concepts such as collaborative intelligence, democratization and decentralization of information are becoming increasingly ingrained in our virtual culture.

According to Freitas (2006), a consultant and project manager, Web 2.0 is a reality because it evolves the way users relate to each other in the virtual world. It would be the change from a Web that only provided information to a model in which users collaborate, give their opinions and organize information on the Internet.

According to Alves (2006), Web 2.0 content can also be partially collaborative. Stores like Submarino and Amazon, for example, as well as providing product prices and information on how the company works, open up topics for users to write reviews and ratings. By exchanging information with other users, people are motivated to buy a certain type of product or not.

The important thing is that there is no technological innovation in Web 2.0, but only the reuse of established technologies with a new approach. (SAMPAIO, 2007, p.9)

2.4 VIRAL MARKETING MEDIA

According to Telles (2007), the term Viral Marketing is linked to strategies that lead people to proliferate messages, information and applications in a natural way, like a kind of virus.

The following are some of the resources that are used to attract audiences in the media, using the development of digital games.

2.4.1. BLOG

The term Blog comes from an English word made up of the words Web, which represents an Internet page, and log, which means logbook. Over time, the word was shortened to Blog and the big difference between a Blog and an institutional website, apart from the fact that the most recent content is always above the oldest, is the interactivity and the space for comments. (TERRA, 2008, p.71)

According to Terra (2008, p.73), corporate blogs are a communication channel between the company and its public, which allows for a bilateral and more informal conversation, and the tool can be exploited in the corporate world as a relationship, dissemination, third-party endorsement of corporate reputation and image and dialog.

"The impact of this rapid dissemination of ideas and opinions can be seen as a problem or a great opportunity for organizations - all it takes is for the company to be attentive to what happens on the Internet, without ever ignoring its possible negative points. Corporate blogs are more than a trend; they are a reality that is here to stay, as is the need for companies to adapt to it." (BEGARA, 2006)

Corporate blogs are basically divided into two types: **external** and **internal**.

A) EXTERNAL

For Terra (2008, p.74), external corporate blogs are those that the public company creates for anyone to access on the Internet, with the purpose of external interaction, whether as a communication channel, or brand reinforcement, feedback for product development, crisis management, public relations, media relations, strategic positioning, etc.

Terra (2008, p.75) says that the external blog is not a substitute for the traditional web page, and states that the difference between the web page and the blog is that the former works like a library, where the customer learns about the company, and in the latter, the customer "talks" to the company, as well as consulting it.

B) INTERNS

Begara (2006) says that internal corporate blogs are generally used as a tool for interaction between employees. It is a very efficient way of laying the foundations for internal communication, managing knowledge and projects and reinforcing human resources initiatives.

We can highlight two games that TV Rede Globo's Bola nas Costas blog makes available for the public to interact with the proposed theme (Sport), thus increasing the time spent on the site. The games can be seen in Figure 1 and Figure 2.

Figura 1: Game Caça Taça - Rede Globo[1] , allows Internet users to draw teams that will be champions of the championships that are taking place.

<hr>

1 The Caça Taça game can be accessed at the following link:
http://globoesporte.globo.com/platb/bolanascostas/category/games/

Figura 2: Canhao do Brasileirao - Rede Globo[2] , allows internet users to play at hitting the ducks that correspond to the competing teams in the Brazilian Championship.

2.4.2. SOCIAL NETWORKS

According to the G1 website (2008), a social network is a relationship established between individuals who share the same interests in the same environment. On the Internet, social networks are known as online communities, which allow Internet users to communicate and share information.

A social network is defined by a set of two elements: actors (people, institutions or groups; the nodes of the network) and their connections (interactions or social ties) (WASSERMAN and FAUST 1994; DEGENNE and FORSÉ 1999). A network is thus a metaphor for observing patterns of connection within a social group, based on the connections established between the various actors. The network approach thus focuses on social structure, where it is not possible to isolate the actors or their connections. (RECUERO, 2009, p.24)

As social networks on the Internet have expanded the possibilities for connections, they have also expanded the ability of these groups to disseminate information. In the offline space, news or information only spreads on the web through conversations between

---

2 The game Canhão do Brasileirão can be accessed at the following link:
   http://globoesporte.globo.com/platb/bolanascostas/2010/08/31/canhao-do-brasileirao/

people. On online social networks, this information is much more amplified, reverberated, discussed and passed on. Thus, we say that these networks have given people more voice, more value-building and greater potential for spreading information. It is therefore these webs of connections that spread information, give people a voice, build different values and give access to this type of value. (RECUERO, 2009, p.25)

According to (RECUERO, 2009, p.30), connections are the main focus of the study of social networks, because the changes that occur in ties and connections are what structure the behavior of the social network.

We can highlight the marketing campaign that the game Colheita Feliz promoted on Orkut, including Lacta's MINI BIS among the purchase items, to publicize the launch of the product.

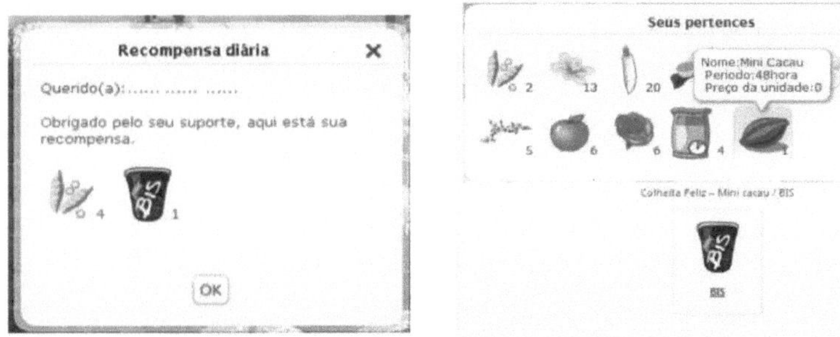

Figura 3:   Image of the Happy Harvest Game (reproduction)

The campaign for the game Colheita Feliz (Happy Harvest), which is a fever on Orkut (with almost 20 million players), managed to exceed expectations and cause a lot of controversy in various media, with the insertion of advertising in the game.

Figure 4: Image of the game Colheita Feliz (reproduction)

3. GAME DEVELOPMENT

The constant search for new forms of promotion has led companies to invest in the use of new technologies. It is now common to develop electronic games to promote a specific brand.

With the development of these applications, companies are able to provide their large audiences with a high level of interactivity, as well as the low cost of producing and publicizing these applications compared to traditional means of publicizing and marketing.

Steven Johnson (2006, p. 54) points out that in the last 50 years, we have had to learn to deal with an explosion of media, technologies and interfaces, from the television remote control to the Internet. And each new form of media - especially the visual and interactive ones - implies an implicit challenge to our brains: we have to explore the logic of the new interface, follow the clues, understand the relationships.

Looking at the volume of work showing the consequences and influences of gaming on players' behavior, skills and cognition, both the positive and negative aspects of gaming on people's education, Baki et al (2008) concluded that "video games are both beneficial and harmful to students' learning process".

3.1 IDEAS

Ideas for developing a game can arise from a small concept in a variety of ways:

- an original concept presented by a company employee;

- an original concept established by an outsider;

- a sequel to an existing game;

- an adaptation based on a character from an existing game;

- a game based on an existing character or story (such as characters from movies, TV or comics);

- a simulation of other games (such as board games or card games);

- a game aimed at a specific demographic;

- a simulation of a real-world event;

- a game developed to take advantage of a specific gaming platform (such as the Internet or an advanced interactive gaming system). (TYSON, 2007, p. 198)

For this reason, care must be taken to ensure that unripe ideas are not eliminated. The creative process can be facilitated by questions such as: "What is the aim of the game?",

"What will the player have to do?", "How will they do it?", "What will make this game fun?" (PERUCIA et al., 2005, p. 82).

As soon as an idea is accepted by the company as being a viable game, a pre-production team is assembled to begin transforming the idea into a complete game. (TYSON, 2007, p. 92)

3.2 TARGET AUDIENCE

According to Perucia et al. (2005, p. 65), a game should not be designed to appeal to all types of audience, but rather to entertain the players that the designer knows will play it.

When planning a game, a target audience must be established. The average age of game consumers has changed considerably in recent years, and currently the majority of users are aged between 16 and 25. (REIS JUNIOR; NASSU; JONACK, 2002)

The largest proportion of actual buyers is over 18 years old and it has been found that this age group is home to the most dedicated gamers, and that the tastes of this type of (so-called hardcore) gamer are generally quite different from those of casual gamers. In general, the former have a preference for complex and challenging games, while the latter prioritize lighter and simpler diversions. These statistics contradict the popular idea that games are aimed at children, which was true in the past (REIS JUNIOR; NASSU; JONACK, 2002).

A survey released by Nielsen Entertainment on October 10, 2006, shows that there are more adult women playing video games than men. According to the survey, there are 117 million video game users in the United States, more than half of whom play online (56%) and of these, the majority (64%) are women. In Brazil, there is no similar research, but the industries claim that half of online game purchases are made by women. (CASE, 2004, online)

The themes addressed in games aimed at television audiences represent a little of what McLuhan theorized:

Games are dramatic models of our psychological lives, and serve to release particular tensions (MCLUHAN, 1964, p. 265-266).

This approach to identifying the target audience for an electronic game was taken by the SBT website in 2009, when it launched a game that simulates changing hair in reference to the Eliana show - Beleza Revelada. The aim of this game was to promote the program and bring it closer to the target audience, which is made up of young people aged between 15 and 25.

This gamble to publicize the program by means of an electronic game worked perfectly, as the site's audience grew considerably after the game's launch, according to the broadcaster's press release. The game can be seen in Figure 5.

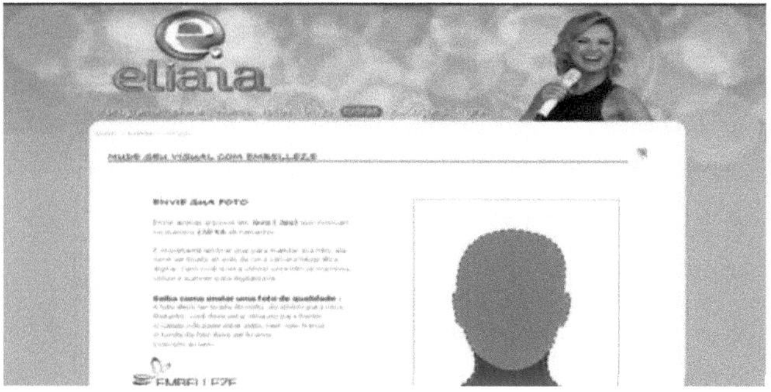
Figure 5: Game Faça seu Cabelo - Eliana

3.3 GAME DESIGN DOCUMENT

This is a report developed by the design company that includes all the information and details for the smooth running of the game project. This document contains the project's market objectives, the results of player research, deadlines and other information. With the Game Design Document in hand, the game designer can make quicker and more efficient decisions, as it contains important information about the market that helps in the search for good results (AZEVEDO et al., 2005, p. 102). The level of detail in the document is so great that it becomes very laborious and exhausting to write (PERUCIA et al., 2005, p. 67).

Game Design is an extension of design practice and means game structural design or game project (CURTI, 2006).

Game Design is the stage of the game development process that determines the details of the gameplay functionality (also called gameplay), the choices that the player will have within the virtual world of the game, as well as the ramifications that their choices will give rise to, what the conditions of victory and defeat will be, how the game will be controlled and the Information that the player should receive (PERUCIA et al., 2005, p. 75).

The game *The Legend of Zelda, The Wind Waker,* produced for the Gamecube console, is a case of well thought-out game design. Nintendo spent three years planning and only eight months programming. The result is an absolutely fantastic game (PERUCIA et all., 2005, p. 88).

3.4 PLANNING A GAME

Like any other software, the production of a game requires the adoption of a development process. (CLUA; BITTENCOURT, 2005, p.107)

Game developers don't take too kindly to a period of planning, as they always want to put a fantastic idea into practice as quickly as possible. Without good planning, developers start a process called *code like hell,* which results in high levels of rework, increased costs and even the extinction of the project due to the drastic changes that occur during the game's production. (PERUCIA et al., 2005, p. 88)

Therefore, the more time that is invested (not wasted) during the planning phase of a game, the greater the ability to have a complete view of the product and the entire development cycle, which certainly allows problems to be anticipated and solved more efficiently. (PERUCIA et al., 2005, p. 154)

4. GALICIAN TV PROJECT

Television is in most Brazilian homes, distracting people, entertaining them and, most of the time, interfering in the way they think, act and relate to the world. Faced with this situation, TV stations are looking for new ways to publicize specific programs, such as *reality shows,* which are used to attract audiences who are inserted in other media.

Among the media that have been integrated with TV in recent years, the internet and social networks stand out. To gain credibility and attract new viewers, broadcasters are investing heavily in building their portals and creating communication channels with their audiences.

According to Kotler, marketing is present in all means of communication where we can attract customers' desires:

Marketing is human activity aimed at satisfying needs and desires through processes of exchange (KOTLER, 1980, p. 15).

One of the bets on the trend to individualize communication, promoting broadcasters' marketing and integrating internet users with TV, is the creation of electronic games, due to the interactivity they provide, as well as the segmentation possibilities.

Therefore, technological means of communication, especially game development, can be used as a resource to publicize the program, transforming the experience that Internet users will have when playing the application, contributing to loyalty and motivating them to watch the program that is being promoted with the advertising campaign.

This feature can be seen in the game 1 Against 100 Online, as shown in Figure 6.

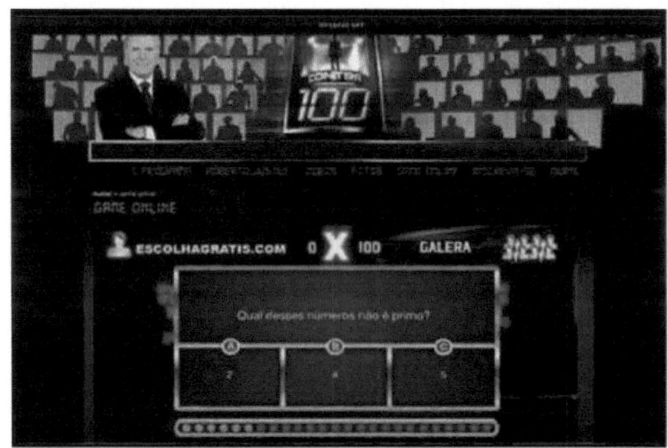

Figure 6: Game 1 against 100 Online[3]

The attractiveness of games, the interactivity they provide, the segmentation possibilities and the low cost of distribution are some of the advantages that games bring to television advertising.

According to a survey of 1,350 gamers conducted by Activision and marketing consultancy Nielsen, the majority of gamers said they were in favor of including advertising in games because it creates the illusion of a real world, providing more credible entertainment. (AGÊNCIA ESTADO, 2009)

We believe that social networks linked to the development of electronic games can promote the growth and expansion of the broadcaster's brand as a whole.

1 .1 THE ROLE OF GAMES IN GENERATING TELEVISION AUDIENCES

Cabrai (2004) refers to the disciplining nature of electronic games and their impact on the formation of subjectivity, a relevant aspect in childhood. Currently, it is "children who, ever earlier, participate in and suffer the social and emotional reality of the adult world, at the same time as they replace the world of creative fantasy with the world of simulacra".

Both games and certain television programs help us to think. According to Steven Johnson (2006), the whole intellectual benefit of playing games comes from this fundamental virtue, because we learn how to think and, in the end, we learn how to make good decisions. These decisions are exercised, according to the author, during the long hours spent in front of the computer, because these forms of entertainment are stimulating cognitive exercises.

Electronic games reproduce reality using colors, images and movements and often inform us about the world, remaking it, transforming it into a spectacle that allows us to recreate (interact) with part of this virtual reality (MRECH, 1997, p. 62).

In 2009, SBT's website promoted a spectacle of integrating fantasy with reality, in line with Mrech's thinking, by developing a game that gave internet users the chance to feel like they were taking part in a campaign like the telethon. This is a big step, as it helps the broadcaster create an identity with internet users. This campaign can be seen in Figure 7.

---

3 Game 1 contra 100 Online : It can be accessed on the SBT website, available at the following link: http://www.sbt.com.br/umcontracem/gameonline

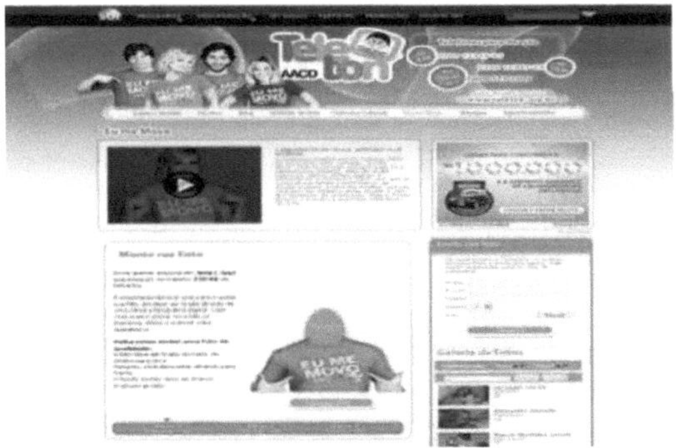

Figure 7: Game Eu Me Movo (Telethon / SBT)

At the beginning of this third millennium, in which technology dominates all spaces, from the public to the private (ATMs, sophisticated household electronics such as small robots, digital TV, cell phones, palmtops, refrigerators, microwaves, washing machines), games seem to emerge as "natural teachers" (GENTILE and ANDERSON, 2005, p. 172).

Among the researchers who have written about the influence of games, there are those who defend the influence of this experience on cognitive processes and their subsequent development, such as Greenfield (1988, 1996), who points to games as stimulators of cognitive development and reasoning.

In 2008, SBT launched an online game called "Jogo dos Artistas", used as a stimulant to promote the SBT brand on the internet. The broadcaster's strategy was to attract both television and online audiences.

To make this possible, a draw was held among the more than 1 million players who managed to match 3 similar images of the broadcaster's artists on the same line, offering a prize of a car worth 25,000 reais. The image of the game can be seen in Figure 8.

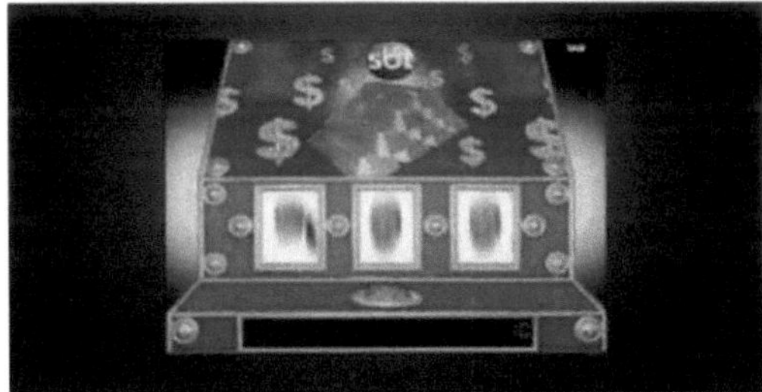

Figure 8: Jogo dos Artistas (SBT)

The game, in general, among its characteristics, has the ability to create order and to be order itself, since the game "introduces into the confusion of life and the imperfection of the world a temporary and limited perfection, it demands a supreme and absolute order: the slightest disobedience to it 'spoils the game', depriving it of its own character and of any value." (HUIZINGA, 1993, p. 13)

In reference to the program "Você se Lembra", SBT has developed a game that tests the memory of internet users. This was a way of attracting virtual viewers to watch the program on television. The game can be seen in Figure 9.

Figure 9: Memory Test - Do you remember (SBT)

4.2 BRIEF HISTORY OF THE COMPANY

According to the TV GALEGA website, at the end of 1996 and the beginning of 1997, journalist Altair Carlos Pimpao and his son, engineer Carlos Eduardo Pimpâo, decided to share the idea of a community video project with businessmen from the BTV Cable Television System in Blumenau. The idea became Blumenau's first community broadcaster: TV GALEGA - CANAL 7, founded on March 3, 1997.

Thus was born a broadcaster that today is part of the daily lives of thousands of people, bringing information, entertainment, culture and instruction. Its name - GALEGA - was inspired by the nickname by which women of German origin, the nationality of Blumenau's founders, are known in the region.

According to institutional information, the station has a modern television concept inspired by the so-called "public access channels". It airs reports and news that reflect the real pulse of a region in continuous development, its difficulties, its problems, its achievements, in short, its day-to-day life. There, citizens can express themselves, feel represented and communicate with their representatives.

TV Galega plays the role of an electronic forum, in which everyone can share information with their community, discuss projects and ideas, present demands. The neighborhoods, the city, the region are all present in its news and reports, always with the viewer in mind.

22

It also represents an advantageous space for publicizing companies, products and services, given the significant number of viewers it reaches (138,000/Feb-00), just locally, without counting the audience from other places, who are Internet users.

One of the station's distinguishing features, according to its institutional website, is its varied and interactive programming, which is made not just for the viewers, but with the viewers, which is why it has been described as "The Image of the City".

4.3 CHOICE OF TOOL AND SYSTEM STRUCTURE

The structure of the system follows the line of games developed for internet browsing. Adobe Flash was used as a tool, with Object Oriented modeling.

According to Guimarâes et. all.(2007, p.15), Adobe Flash has a familiar environment, providing support from the point of view of abstraction and a notion of how objects will be presented in relation to other tools that are also used in the market for game development.

At this stage, a game was developed to be published on the TV Galega website, integrated with social networks to promote the program and the broadcaster's website.

A soccer match was taken as an example for the development of this application, where the aim is to score as many ambassadorial goals as possible in order to publish the result on social networks such as Twitter and show the score to all your friends. The documentation and structure of the project can be seen in the GDD - Game Document Designer.

4.4 GDD - GAME DOCUMENT DESIGNER

Schedule for the Production Stages of the **"BLUMENAU ESPORTES"** game[i]

Stage
1. Planning and gathering materials for layout development
2. Layout creation
3. Layout approval
4. Flash editing
5. Video editing - opening of the game
6. Flash programming
7. Finalization / Proofreading
8. Testing and Validation

PROJECT DATA

Name: Blumenau Esportes

Type: Electronic game that simulates the Blumenau Sports Program and allows users to have fun with some sports.

Development time : 2 months

Gameplay Overview:

The game promotes the Blumenau Esportes program. *In* it, the player can interact with the presenter and have fun playing soccer.

Target Audience:

This game is aimed at the target audience of casual gamers *(young people between the ages of 10 and 15)*.

Look & Feel *(Expectation of the experience generated with the game)***:**

In the age of interactive communication, the Internet is proving to be an excellent tool for publicizing services and integrating people with the same interests.   Online games are being used to inform, raise awareness and publicize services in a more dynamic and attractive way.   Actions such as building electronic games help to strengthen the relationship with the public.

1.05 - *Advergame* **references :**

There's nothing better to test a brand or product than to put them into games. This is the conclusion of a survey conducted by game producer Activision and marketing consultancy Nielsen with 1,350 male gamers aged between 13 and 44. The majority said they were in favor of including advertising in games, because "it creates the illusion of a real world and gives the entertainment greater credibility". (Agência Estado, 2009)   Electronic games have always been associated with children and adolescents, but this is an outdated view of the current market. A survey carried out by the ESA (Entertainment Software Association) showed that 69% of heads of household in the United States play electronic games on computers or video games (ENTERTAINMENT, 2006).   According to IBOPE Inteligência (IBOPE, 2005), online games account for 4.1% of the total time spent using the Internet in Brazilian households, a percentage very close to that of the United States with 7.2% and higher than that of Spain with 3.8%.

We can see the use of *In-Game Advertising in* the figure below:

Figure 10: Screenshot of the FIFA 07 game for Xbox 360

GAME ENVIRONMENT

Scenery:

The game's plot takes place in the Galician TV studios and on the soccer pitch.

Score:

The player will have 1 minute to try to make as many embassies as possible. Each correct embassy scores the player 10 points.

With each error, i.e. if the buoy hits the ground, the count is restarted.

At the end of the game, the highest score is counted in the *ranking.*

Sound effects:

Environment:

The game should have audio when the player is kicking the ball and making the boxes, and a soundtrack throughout the game.

Movement / Play:

The player will use the mouse to interact with the game.

Graphic Art:

Since this is a webgame and the architecture we will adopt will load all the information and resources at once (during the Loading Screen), we should develop material with good graphics and sound quality but that does not exceed the size of most webgames.

The resolution of the game for development will be 550 *pixels* X 450 *pixels.*

ROTEIRO

***Loading* screen:**

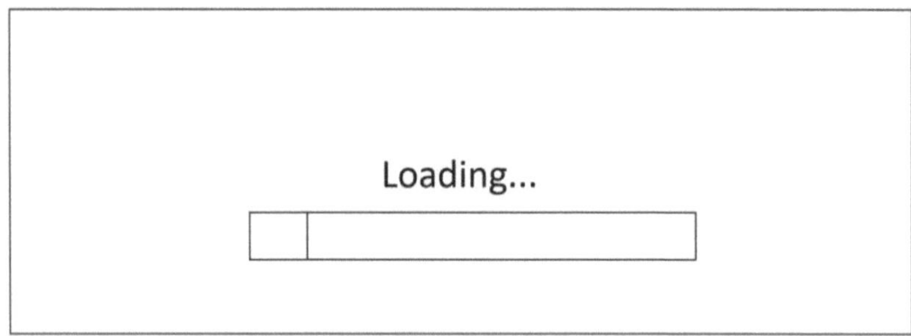

Game *splash* with menu and options:

Menu reference : http://www.cocacolazero.com/index.jsp#/czvideos/

Help (How to Play):

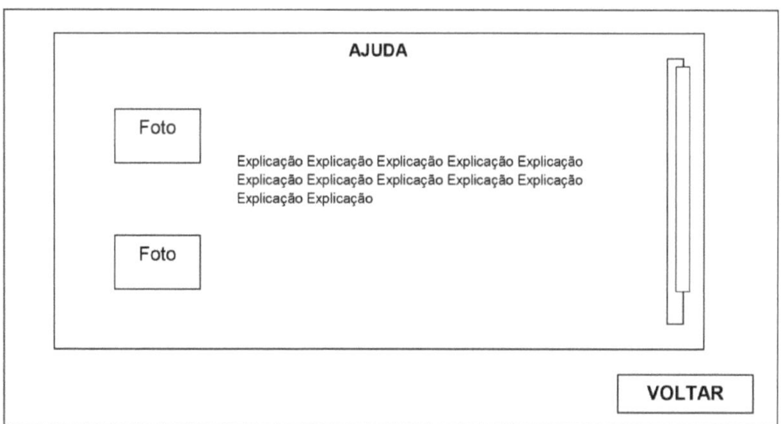

Share:

SHARE

URL

http://www.tvgalega.com.br/

Promote the game on social media.

| Twitter | Facebook | My Space | Delicious |

VOLTAR

Share Reference: http://redeglobo.globo.com/tv_globo/noticias/0,,mul110 8307-16162,00-teste+wilson+caetano+descubra+quem+voce+e+em+forcatarefa.html

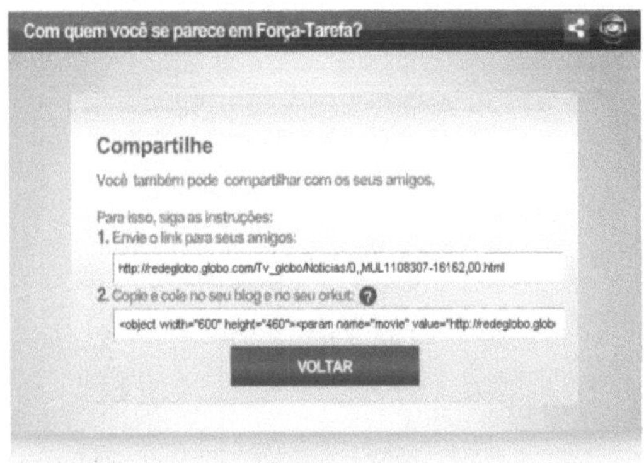

Play:

Save the result in the communities:

Share your score on social media

You did very well in the TV Galega game Show your friends your score

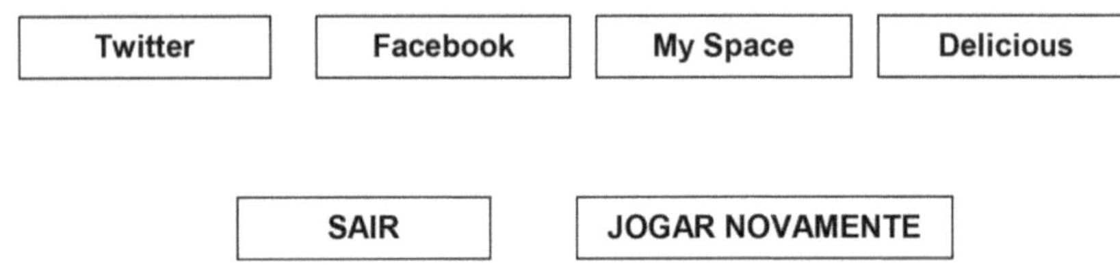

GAME SCREENS

Game start:

Select the Share option:

Share layout:

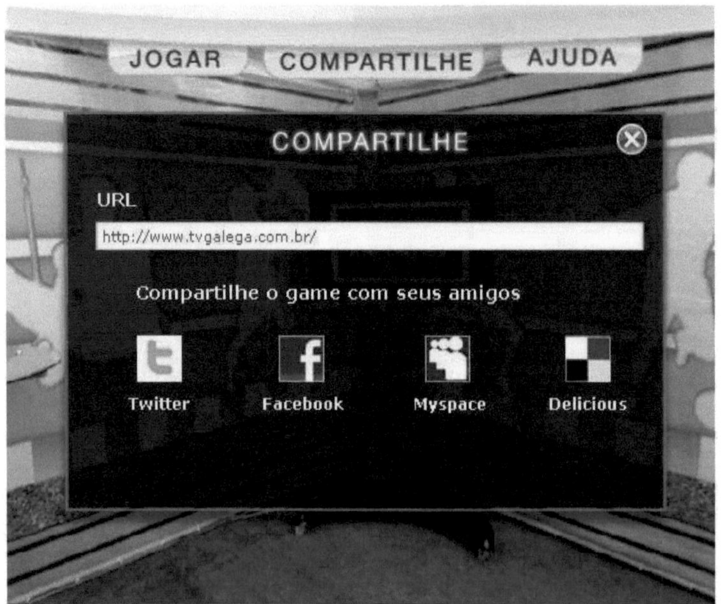

Select the Help option:

Help:

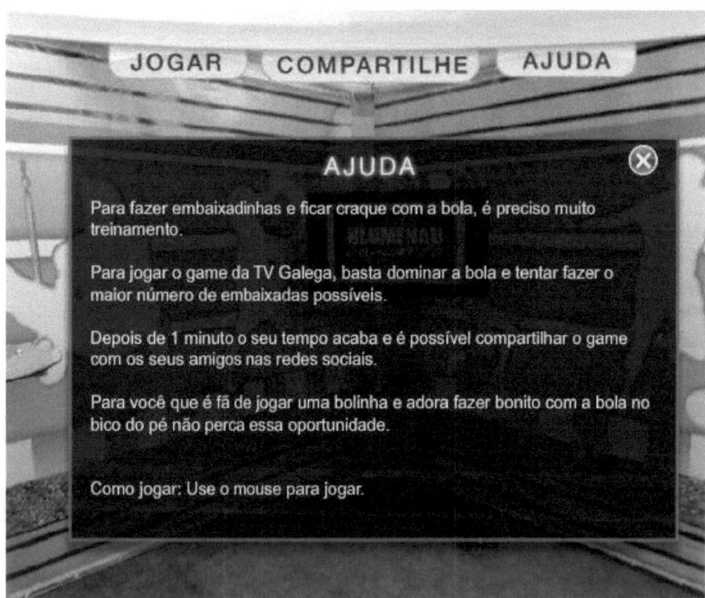

Game Opening Video:

Game's main screen:

Final Game Message:

Facebook screen demo:

Twitter screen demo:

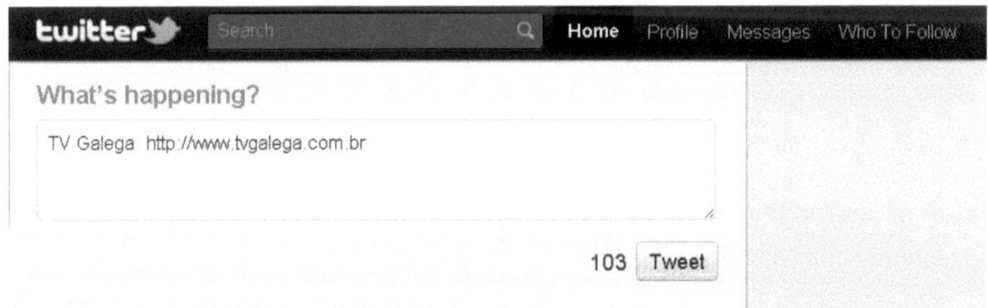

4.5 BUSINESS PLAN

The Business Plan deals with the commercial aspects of the project, such as differentials and reasons for getting investment.

Executive Summary:

The global games market is booming, and Brazil is no exception, with an increasing number of international companies setting up bases in our territory at the same time as national companies are being born and succeeding.

With a differentiated proposal, both commercially and technologically, presenting a unique theme and possibilities for interaction, the Embaixadinhas game has all the qualities needed to attract the program's viewers.

The image of the program can be seen in Figure 11.

Figure 11: Image from the Blumenau Esportes program (TV Galega).

Product

An electronic game that simulates the Blumenau Sports Program and allows users to have fun with some sports.

Product Summary

The game promotes the Blumenau Esportes program. In it, the player can interact with the presenter and have fun with embassies.

Quality System

Using *debug* and *quality assurance* teams, products will be reviewed during development, ensuring that errors are corrected and avoiding future problems. 46

tures.

Research and Development

The Adobe Flash games market (one of the best creative environments for producing interactive and expressive content) is booming in Brazil, with widespread technology and a development platform that is quick to learn, effective and agile to produce, requiring little time between project and final product.

Technological edge

The game will be made available on the internet, with the aim of increasing the audience and dwell time on the company's institutional website.

Records

All intellectual property registrations and all topics related to the game, such as its logo and characters, have already been duly registered by TV Galega.

Strategic Alliances

Support from TV Galega for the development of the TCC.

Enterprise - Company Data

TV GALEGA LTDA

Rua: Uruguai n°124

ZIP CODE: 89050-060

Blumenau - SC Tele-

fax:(047) 3326-7788

Management data

Altair Carlos Pimpao, General Director of TV Galega

Business Definition

TV GALEGA, which follows a modern television concept inspired by the so-called "public access channels", broadcasts reports and news that reflect the true pulse of a region in continuous development, its difficulties, its problems, its achievements, in short, its day-to-day life. There, citizens can express themselves, feel represented and communicate with their representatives.

Vision

Realization of increasingly innovative projects, investing in the creativity of the creators to create games that captivate gamers.

S.W.O.T. Analysis

Opportunities: Optimism in relation to new games produced in Brazil, search for games via the internet, large audience reach via the internet.

Threats: Saturation of online gaming offers.

Internal Environment: Strengths and Weaknesses

Strengths: Low cost of time and money in development, optimized and agile implementation, portability, creativity, new intellectual properties, games with approaches to subjects known and admired by developers.

Weaknesses: Small team, little monetary investment, lack of reference as a basis for production.

Human Resources

Only the creator of the project.

Physical Resources

1 computer. Broadband connection.

Technological resources

Operating system (Windows: XP, Vista, 7 or Linux or Mac OS).

Office tools (Word, Excel, PowerPoint).

Adobe tools (Flash, Fireworks, Photoshop, Premiere).

Current Situation - Market

Currently, there is a growing interest in *advergames* (games with an advertising slant). According to Jairo Margatho, marketing manager at developer Délirus Entertainment, advertising agencies already recognize *advergames as* an interactive media that has a potential audience that spends at least four hours on the computer (ABRAGAMES, 2005).

Target Audience Identification

Mainly men between the ages of 10 and 17, who like soccer and watch the sports program Blumenau Esportes.

Market trends

Games that are simpler and easier to learn, but at the same time hold the player's attention.

Sales projections

The main aim of developing the game is to increase the audience of the company's institutional website.

Strategies and Objectives - Marketing

Investment in publicity in all related media, such as specialized magazines and websites with advertisements.

The use of Portuguese as the default language in the software allows it to reach a wide range of users, since its main focus market is Brazil, the same country as the developer.

Distribution Channels

Distribution via the broadcaster's own website.

Online Promotion

Official website and development blog.

Promote the launch of the game on social networks (Orkut, Facebook and Twitter).

Finance

Financial plan for the project.

Initial Investment

Own capital to buy computers, software and equipment.

Monthly costs

The contract to use the TV Galega brand and property will not cost you anything.

Schedule

Schedule for the Production Stages of the **BLUMENAU ESPORTES** game

Stage
1. Planning and gathering materials for layout development
2. Layout creation
3. Layout approval
4. Layout structuring in Adobe Flash
5. Video editing - opening of the game
6. Flash programming
7. Finalization / Proofreading
8. Testing and Validation

5. CONCLUSION

It was possible to complete the development of the proposed games. During this process, it became clear that the companies believe in the potential of using games to promote their brands, given their consent to use the brand and the support and engagement of the companies' marketing teams in creating specific artwork for the games, as well as analyzing the preliminary versions and proposing suggestions and improvements.

TV Galega understood that developing games can help promote the brand and help the company in its line of business.

6. ANNEXES (COPIES OF CONTRACTS AND EXCERPTS OF SOURCE CODE)

6.1 AUTHORIZATION CONTRACT WITH GALICIAN TV FOR THE DEVELOPMENT OF THE **project.**

TV GALGGA

Blumenau, March 3rd, 2011

lime. Mr.

Marcelo Henrique dos Santos

Rua Âlvaro Mathias, 170 Jardim Veneza

08715-490 Mogi das Cruzes - Sâo Paulo

Dear Sir:

AUTHORIZATION LETTER

We are very pleased with your proposal to develop, free of charge, an electronic game based on a program on our station, which is celebrating its 14th anniversary today.

We'll be very proud to have your post-graduation work in Games Production and Programming at Senac University in our hands at a later date.

This is to give you permission to use audio and video in the production of your game on the Blumenau Esportes program.

Altair Carlos Pimpao Managing Director

TV GALEGA LTDA.

Rua Uruguai, 124 - PontaAguda - CEP 89050-060 - Blumenau - Santa Catarina
Phone: (47) 3326-7788 - www.tvgalega.com.br - E-mail: comercial.tv@tvgalega.com.br

6.2 EXCERPT FROM THE SOURCE CODE OF THE GAME DEVELOPED FOR TV GALEGA - "FAÇA EMBAIXADINHAS".

```
var velocidadex:Number          = Math.random()*30;
var velocidadey:Number          = Math.random()*30;
var bordadireita:Number         = stage.stageWidth;
var bordaesquerda:Number        = 0;
var tetotela:Number             = 0;
var chaotela:Number             = stage.stageHeight;
var gravidade:Number            = 2;
var atrito:Number               = .98;
var elasticidade:Number         = .9;
var arrastando:Boolean          = false;
var xvelho:Number               = 0;
var yvelho:Number               = 0;
var placar:uint                 = 0;
var valorMaximo:uint            = 0;

function init():void{
        MovieClip(root).Verifica(valorMaximo, placar);
        botao_btn.addEventListener(MouseEvent.CLICK, onMouseClick_botao);
}

function keyFrame2():void{
        if (!arrastando) {

                this.x += velocidadex;
                this.y += velocidadey;
                velocidadey = (velocidadey * atrito) + gravidade;
                velocidadex *= atrito;

                /*---------- Move em X --------------*/
                if (this.x + this.width/2 > bordadireita) {
                        this.x = bordadireita - this.width/2;
                        velocidadex =-velocidadex*elasticidade;
                }
                if(this.x - this.width/2 < bordaesquerda) {
                        this.x = bordaesquerda + this.width/2;
                        velocidadex=-velocidadex*elasticidade;
                }

                /*---------- Move em Y --------------*/
                if (this.y + this.height/2 > chaotela) {
                        Func_Apito ();
                        this.y = chaotela - this.height/2;
                        velocidadey=-velocidadey*elasticidade;
                        if (placar > valorMaximo){
                                valorMaximo = placar;
```

```actionscript
                                placar = 0;
                        }else{
                                placar = 0;
                        }
                }

                if(this.y - this.height/2 < tetotela) {
                        this.y = tetotela + this.height/2;
                        velocidadey=-velocidadey*elasticidade;
                }
        }else{
                velocidadex = this.x - xvelho;
                velocidadey = this.y - yvelho;
                xvelho = this.x;
                yvelho = this.y;
        }

        MovieClip(root).Verifica(valorMaximo,placar);
}

var audio_Embaixada:Embaixada                    = new Embaixada();

var Channel1:SoundChannel                  = new SoundChannel();

function Func_Apito() {
        Channel1 =  audio_Embaixada.play();
}

function onMouseClick_botao(e:MouseEvent):void{
        placar += 10;
        arrastando = true;

        if(Math.random() * 1 > .5){
                velocidadex = Math.random() * 10;
        }else{
                velocidadex = - Math.random() * 20;
        }

        if(velocidadey - Math.random() * 20 > .5){
                velocidadey = - Math.random() * 20;
        }else{
                velocidadey = - Math.random() * 30;
        }

        arrastando = false;
}

function onMouseDown_botao(e:MouseEvent):void{
        this.startDrag();
        arrastando = true;
```

```actionscript
}

function onMouseUp_botao(e:MouseEvent):void{
	this.stopDrag();
	arrastando = false;
}

init();


			colorTransformPincel.color = cor;
		cursor.ponta_mc.transform.colorTransform = colorTransformPincel;
			break;
		case 'color27_btn' :
			cor = 0x2D3798;
			colorTransformPincel.color = cor;
		cursor.ponta_mc.transform.colorTransform = colorTransformPincel;
			break;
		case 'color28_btn' :
			cor = 0x6C3394;
			colorTransformPincel.color = cor;
		cursor.ponta_mc.transform.colorTransform = colorTransformPincel;
			break;
	}
}
```

7. REFERENCES

ABRAGAMES. **The electronic game development industry in Brazil**. 2005. Available at: <http://www.abragames.com>. Accessed on: April 12, 2011.

STATE AGENCY. **Gamers approve of advertising in games**. Available at: <http://www.forumpcs.com.br/noticia.php?b=140419>. Accessed on March 23, 2010.

ALVES JR, G. **What the video with Cicarelli has to tell us**. Webinsider, September 21, 2006. Available at: <http://webinsider.uol.com.br/index.php/2006/09/2l/ oque-o-video-de-cicarelli-tem-a--nos-dizer/>. Accessed on: May 10, 2011.

ALVES, L. **Game over: electronic games and violence**. 2004. Thesis (Doctorate in Education). Postgraduate Program in Education. Federal University of Bahia, 2004.

AZEVEDO, E. et al. **Development of 3D games and applications in virtual reality**. Rio de Janeiro: Elsevier, 2005. 319 p.

BAKI, R.; LENG, E.; ALI, W.; ROSNAINI, M.; MOHN. H., **The perspective of six Malaysian students on playing video games**: beneficial or detrimental? US- China Education Review, 2008, v. 5, serial n. 48. Available at < http://www.eric.ed.gov/PDFS/ED503878.pdf >. Accessed on July 5, 2011.

BEGARA, T. **Blogs invade the corporate world** (05/05/2006).

Available at: <http://www.catho.com.br/jcs/inputer_view.phtml?id=7920&print=1>. Accessed on: April 12, 2011.

BELINE, R. Variaçâo linguistica. In: FIORIN, José Luiz (Org.). **Introduçâo à linguistica**. 3. ed. Sao Paulo: Contexto, 2004.

BRAGA, D. **Hipertexto**: questões de produção e de leitura. Published in 2004. Available at: <http:www.gel.org.br>. Accessed on: April 12, 2011.

CABRAL, F. Interview. In: **4ª World Summit on Media for Children and Adolescents.** Rio de Janeiro: Multirio, 2004. Available at:

<http://www.riosummit2004.com.br/entrevista.asp?id_noticias=401&idioma=por&foru m=>. Accessed on: March 23, 2010.

CASE, S. **Women in games**. January 12, 2004. Available at: <http://www.microsoft.com/brasil/windowsxp/using/games/learnmore/womeningames. mspx>. Accessed on March 23, 2010.

CLARK, W.; PRIOLLI, G. **O campeão de audiência**. Sao Paulo: Nova Cultural/Best

Seller, 1991.

CLUA, E. W. G.; BITTENCOURT J. R. **Development of 3D Games**: conception, design and programming. Available at:

<http://www.unisinos.br/_diversos/congresso/sbc2005/_dados/anais/pdf/arq0286.pdf>.

Accessed on: April 12, 2011.

CRAWFORD, C. **The art of computer design**. 1982. Available at:

<http://www.vancouver.wsu.edu/fac/peabody/game-book/Coverpage.html>. Accessed on: April 12, 2011.

CUNHA, J. L. **Digital marketing**: do you use it in your business? Available at <http://www.e-negociodigital.com.br/pdf/MarketingDigital.pdf>. Accessed on April 26, 2011.

CURTI, M. M. **Concepts and technologies in the development of electronic games**. 2006. 84 p. Course Conclusion Paper, Information Systems - UNIFEV, Centro Universitàrio de Votuporanga, Votuporanga, 2006.

EISNER, Will, **Quadrinhos e arte seqüencial.** 2^a ed. Sao Paulo: Martins Fontes, 1995.

FERREIRA, A. B. H. **Mini Aurélio século XXI**: o minidicionârio da lingua portu- guesa. Rio de Janeiro: Nova Fronteira, 2002.

FERREIRA, I. G. et al. **Dicionârio brasileiro de media**. 2a ed. Sao Paulo: Mercado Global, 1996. p. 34.

ONLINE   ONLINE. **Understand what WEB 2.0 is**. Available at: <

http://www1.folha.uol.com.br/folha/informatica/ult124u20173.shtml>. Accessed on: April 12, 2011.

FRANCO, E. **Hqtrônicas:** do suporte papel a rede Internet. Sao Paulo: Editora An- nablume, 2004. p.138

FREITAS, R. A. **Web 2.0 strengthens knowledge management concepts and presents new challenges**. Available at: <http://www.intranetportal.com.br/colab1/ web20>. Accessed on: May 10, 2011.

G1: What is a social network? Available at: <http://g1.globo.com/Noticias/0,,MUL394839-15524,00.html>. Accessed on: April 12, 2011.

GENTILE , D. A.; ANDERSON, C.; A. **Video games and children.** Available at:

<http://www.psychology.iastate.edu/faculty/caa/abstracts/2005-2009/05ga1.pdf>. Accessed on: March 23, 2010.

GREENFIELD, P. M. **The development of reasoning in the electronic age**: the effects of TV, computers and video games. Sao Paulo: Summus, 1996.

GUIMARÂES, COSTA, SOARES. Rodrigo Laiola, Romualdo M. de Resende, Luiz Fernando Gomes. **Composer**: authoring environment for declarative applications for interactive digital TV. Monograph from the Department of Informatics. PUC Rio. Rio de Janeiro: PUC, 2007.

HIGUCHI, K. K. Super-Homem, Mônica & Cia. In: CITELLI, Adilson (Org.). **Aprender e ensinar com textos não escolares**. 5. ed. Sao Paulo: Cotez, 2002.

HUIZINGA, J. **Homo ludens**: o jogo como elemento da cultura. 4 ed. Sao Paulo: Perspectiva, 1993.

IANNONE, L. R.; IANNONE, R. A. **O mundo das histórias em quadrinhos**. 7. ed. Sao Paulo: Moderna, 1998.

KOTLER, P. **Marketing:** Compact Edition. Sao Paulo: Atlas, 1980.

LÉVY, P. **Cibercultura**. 2. ed. Sao Paulo: Ed. 34, 2000.

LIRA, H. **Comics on the Internet**: an adaptation to the new challenges of digital narrative. Master's dissertation in Arts and Design. Rio de Janeiro. Pontifical Catholic University of Rio de Janeiro. PUC-Rio, 2005. Available at: <www.puc-rio.br>. Accessed on: April 12, 2011.

LOVETRO, J. A. Comics: the complete language. **Communication and Education**. Sao Paulo, n° 2, p. 94-101, Jan./Apr. 1995.

MAURICIO de Sousa celebrates 50 years of his career at the Bienal. Available at: <http://portal.rpc.com.br/gazetadopovo/cadernog/conteudo.phtml?id=923807>. Accessed on: April 12, 2011.

McCLOUD, S. **Reinventing comics**. Sao Paulo: M. Books, 2006.

MCLUHAN, M. **Os meios de comunicação como extensões do homem**. 12. Ed. Sao Paulo: Cultrix, 2002

MISTERAPE. **Advertisement by major companies in the games market**. 2006. Available at: <http://misterape.com.br/news/308/>. Accessed on: April 12, 2011.

MRECH, L. M. The child and the computer: new ways of thinking. In: SANTOS, Santa

Marli P. dos. (Org.) **Brinquedoteca**: o lùdico em diferentes contex- tos. Petrópolis, 1997. p. 62-80.

PEREIRA, H. C. **Web 2.0 doesn't mean anything**. I'm sorry! Available at: <http://www.revolucao.etc.br/archives/web-20-nao-significa-nada-me- sorry> . Accessed on: May 10, 2011.

PERUCIA, A. S. et al. **Development of electronic games:** theory and practice. Sao Paulo: Novatec, 2005. 320 p.

RECUERO, Raquel. **Social Capital**. 2009. Available at: <http://www.compos.org.br/d ata/biblioteca_913.pdf>. Accessed on: April 26, 2011.

REIS JUNIOR, A. S.; NASSU, B. T.; JONACK, M. A. A **study on the development processes of electronic games (games).** Available at <http://www.ademar.org/texts/processo-desenv-games.pdf>. Accessed on July 5, 2011.

SAMPAIO, C. **Web 2.0 and Mashups**: reinventing the Internet. Sao Paulo: Brasport, 2007.

Game Center. Available at <http://www.sbt.com.br>. Accessed on: April 13, 2011.

STEVEN J. Everything bad is good for you. **Thematic Communication, Neurons Collection.** Lisbon: FNAC, Colombo, April, 2006.

TARCIA, L. **Ação, pesquisa e reflexâo sobre a docência na formação do jornalista em tempos de convergência das medias digitais**. 2007, 256 p. Dissertation (Education and Digital Technologies) - Master's Degree in Education, PUC Minas, 2007.

TELLES, A. **Orkut.com:** how you and your company can take advantage of Brazil's largest social networking site. Sâo Paulo: Landscape, 2006.

TERRA, C. F. **Corporate blogs**: fad or trend? Sâo Caetano do Sul, SP: Difusâo Editora, 2008.

Galician TV. Available at: <http://www.tvgalega.com.br/hpn/institucional/index.php>. Accessed on: May 10, 2011.

TYSON, J. **How 3DO creates video games**. 2007. Available at: <http://informatica .hsw.uol.com.br/como-a-3do-cria-videogames.htm>. Accessed on: April 12, 2011.

BARBOSA, A. **Advertising in games will generate US$ 400 million in 2009**. Available at: <http://www.estadao.com.br/tecnologia/intemet/noticias/2006/ jun/19/10.htm>. Accessed on: July 05, 2011.

ENTERTAINMENT SOFTWARE ASSOCIATION. **Essential facts**: about the computer and video game industry. Report created by a market research company, Washington, 2006.

IBOPE. Report analyzes Internet use in Brazil, the United States and Spain. Available at: <http://www.ibope.com.br/calandraweb/servlet/calandrarEdirect?temp=6 &proj=portalibope&pub=t&db=caldb&Comp=loja_materia&docid=4325c3d9d3edc99983 25703e00567fc7>. Accessed on: July 5, 2011.

STATE AGENCY. **Gamers approve of advertising in games**. Available at: <http://blogs.forumpcs.com.br/noticias/2005/12/08/jogadores-aprovam-publicidade-em-games/>. Accessed on: July 5, 2011.

I want morebooks!

Buy your books fast and straightforward online - at one of world's fastest growing online book stores! Environmentally sound due to Print-on-Demand technologies.

Buy your books online at
www.morebooks.shop

Kaufen Sie Ihre Bücher schnell und unkompliziert online – auf einer der am schnellsten wachsenden Buchhandelsplattformen weltweit! Dank Print-On-Demand umwelt- und ressourcenschonend produziert.

Bücher schneller online kaufen
www.morebooks.shop

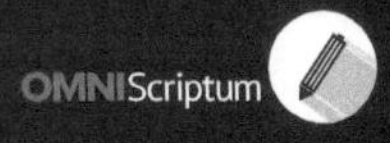

Printed by Books on Demand GmbH, Norderstedt / Germany